Successful
Work Habits
in a week

JANE SMITH

Hodder & Stoughton

A MEMBER OF THE HODDER HEADLINE GROUP

Orders: please contact Bookpoint Ltd, 130 Milton Park, Abingdon, Oxon
OX14 4SB.
Telephone: (44) 01235 827720. Fax: (44) 01235 400454. Lines are open from
9.00–6.00, Monday to Saturday, with a 24 hour message answering service.
Email address: orders@bookpoint.co.uk

British Library Cataloguing in Publication Data
A catalogue record for this title is available from The British Library

ISBN 0 340 848944

First published	2002
Impression number	10 9 8 7 6 5 4 3 2 1
Year	2007 2006 2005 2004 2003 2002

Typeset by SX Composing DTP, Rayleigh, Essex.
Printed in Great Britain for Hodder & Stoughton Educational, a division of
Hodder Headline Plc, 338 Euston Road, London NW1 3BH by
Cox & Wyman Ltd, Reading, Berkshire.

C O N T E N T S

Introduction

Managing a career these days is more than simply 'career planning' or even 'career development'. This is because carefully laid plans can be out of date before the ink is dry. Instead, success depends on developing appropriate attitudes or 'habits'. We are all creatures of habit – how we think and how we behave every second of every day makes us what we are. This book sets out to help you develop the kinds of habits that will make you successful, including adopting an entrepreneurial mindset, working from the heart and developing the ability to commit to change. It also explores the importance of making learning an integral part of your everyday life, taking responsibility for your own motivation and using your time effectively.

If you can do all these things, the final habit – thinking of yourself as a product to be marketed – should come easily. To fulfil your needs you cannot afford to wait for someone to offer you an opportunity. There is no point complaining about your bad luck or about the way the world treats you – you have to be an entrepreneur, you have to be prepared to make things happen.

Be enterprising

Unfortunately, dream jobs rarely come to those who sit and wait; the richest rewards can be claimed only by those who are willing to take charge of their own lives.

To make the most of the many priceless opportunities that wait to be discovered, it is important to get into the habit of thinking like an entrepreneur. This means taking personal responsibility for finding your goals, for learning and for adapting to changed circumstances. Today we are going to explore what it means to be enterprising.

Why do you need to be enterprising?

In the field of employment, many of us can now expect to face substantial change as an almost regular feature of our working lives. You could make a decision to change career. Your company could restructure, downsize, outsource, merge or be bought out at any time. All these initiatives will affect you – your responsibilities, your hours, your boss, even your place of work could change dramatically. Your job could disappear altogether.

A key skill in learning how to survive in this chaos is the ability to recognise and manage change before it takes control of you. If you can adopt the mind-set of an entrepreneur, you will take ownership of the organisation's goals more easily. You will be able to see the big picture rather than focus narrowly on your own job. Your employer will benefit because you will help the organisation to react more quickly to customers' demands. And you will benefit

because you will cease to hold anyone else responsible for what you do or what happens to you. You will be able to look for opportunities to learn, to add value, to make improvements and to fulfil your dreams.

What is an entrepreneur?

Being enterprising is about making your own opportunities. Is to do with getting your needs fulfilled and making the most of what is happening rather than becoming a victim of circumstances. An enterprising person is someone who:

- Displays initiative and solves problems creatively
- Is prepared to change before he or she is forced to by circumstances
- Is not defeated by failure
- Can recognise opportunities when they come along
- Is prepared to take risks

The good news is that these skills and attitudes are not owned only by those who are lucky enough to be born with them – it is possible to learn to be enterprising.

Finding some role models

> 'If I have seen further it is because I have stood on the shoulders of giants.'
>
> Sir Isaac Newton (1676)

One way of developing the skills we need to achieve our goals is to identify one or more role models. If other people are succeeding at something that you would like to do, why struggle to discover the secret of success all by yourself? It is fascinating and fun to learn from other people's lives, and you can even learn a lot from their mistakes! One of my role models is Dawn, an ex-colleague who worked hard, made time to listen to everyone, laughed a lot and never gave up. Another is the Dalai Lama who teaches that there is no point in worrying, because nothing really matters anyway.

Potential role models are all around you. Your own may be famous people, living or dead, or they may be people you work with, friends, or even members of your own family. Analyse what it is that makes them enterprising. What sort of people are they? What have they done? Why have they been successful?

Focusing on other people in this way can help you to see:

- What it is that makes people enterprising
- That enterprising people are not necessarily rich and famous
- That many rich and famous entrepreneurs started off as ordinary mortals
- That it is possible to have some enterprising characteristics without being wholly enterprising in every respect

You are enterprising already . . .

We all look at other people at times in our lives and think that they are somehow cleverer, more efficient, more skilled, more enterprising than we are. There is a tendency to believe that others have some magical qualities that we could never possess; qualities that bring them fulfilment, work, energy, power, success and so on. But if you stop to look closely at what it is that makes people enterprising, you will recognise that you also have some of the skills that they possess.

Look at this list of enterprising qualities and circle six that describe you.

Bold	Effective	Reliable
Confident	Resourceful	Communicative
Determined	Enthusiastic	Decisive
Persistent	Energetic	Adaptable
Creative	Committed	Adventurous
Innovative	Positive	Conscientious
Active	Ambitious	Light-hearted
Inquisitive	Perceptive	Hard working

Now think of times when you have shown that you have some of those qualities – either at work or in your private life. Try to come up with at least one example of a situation where you used them to achieve something you are proud of. 'Success' does not have to be something huge or important. You can give an example of a time when you used your inner resources in a small way.

I hope that this stocktake has made you realise that you already have some enterprising skills, or that there have been occasions when you have been enterprising, possibly without realising it. One of the reasons why you may not have noticed how enterprising you have been is that society places such enormous value on achieving success in terms of work or money. When enterprise is defined in these terms, many people may not recognise the times when they have acted with resourcefulness and enthusiasm. Modest, but heroic enterprises such as organising a self-help group or travelling overseas often remain undervalued.

Once you have recognised where your talents lie, the trick is to look for opportunities to use these skills in your working life. You are capable of getting more of what you want if you start by building on the positive qualities that you already possess.

Confront your fear

> *'If the diver always thought of the shark, he would never lay hands on the pearl.'*
>
> Sadi – Persian poet, 13th century

Fear is an enemy of enterprise. It sucks away at our confidence, weakens our resolve and prevents us from accomplishing what we want in our lives. But the quotation from Sadi tells us all we need know to combat fear. We can choose to try and reach the pearl, or live with regret forever. And the pain that arises from dissatisfaction or lack of fulfilment is often worse than the feeling of fear itself. Of course, evolution has provided us with fear because it stops us from jumping off cliffs or going too close to dangerous animals. But more often than not, there is nothing to fear but fear itself. To make progress we have to confront our fears and distinguish between genuine dangers and situations that we are capable of handling if only we had the confidence to do so.

What are you afraid of? Going for a job interview? Speaking in public? Contacting someone you do not know? The truth is that most of your fears reflect your state of mind rather than anything in the external world. More often than not it comes down to a feeling of inadequacy or a dread of being rejected. If you can conquer these feelings, you can conquer the world.

Many people have found that the way to banish fear is to 'step outside the comfort zone'. This means gently pushing back the boundaries of what you feel you can do, stepping into the unfamiliar territory and staying there for a while until you feel comfortable again. You will be amazed at what you can accomplish when you make yourself do something which has always terrified you in the past. You do not have to parachute out of an aeroplane (not immediately anyway) – a simple thing like making a difficult phone call or speaking in public will make you feel confident enough to push back the boundaries a little more.

Think positively

Unfortunately fear has its own inexorable logic. What we fear frequently comes to pass – often because we make it do so. It follows though, that what we hope for can also happen. Getting out of the self-imposed prison of fear means retraining our thoughts. Do you ever hear a voice in your head that says 'you can't do that' or 'that will never work' or 'you are not good enough'? It would be surprising if you do not because this kind of voice is very strong in most human beings. It is how you react to this voice, whether you listen to it or tell it to be quiet, that makes the difference between success and failure.

The ability to be enterprising is generated by a sense of self-esteem. You will never be able to go after what you want if you really do not believe you deserve it. It follows that your ability to succeed is affected by your beliefs about yourself. For example, if you believe that you cannot use a computer, the result is that you will have difficulty in using a computer. An objective test may prove that you actually have an excellent capacity to learn how to use different computer applications, it is just that you have convinced yourself otherwise.

Our beliefs stem from our experience of life, and we tend to explain events in either a positive or negative way.

- A positive excuse for forgetting something might be 'That's not like me – I must be very absent-minded today'
- A negative excuse for adding some figures up wrongly would go something like 'Trust me to blow it – I'm never any good with numbers'

What happens is that the memory of our behaviour and how we felt on one occasion is carried forward to influence our future experience, either positively or negatively. Facts are not the issue – it is the way that we interpret the facts that dictates the extent of our success or failure in every part of our lives.

Do you tend to interpret your actions positively or negatively, on the whole?

- Note down at least three positive self-beliefs. Then give some examples of behaviour that has given rise to these beliefs
- Now list three self-defeating beliefs about yourself. Again, give an example of the sort of behaviour that supports this belief
- Finally, translate each of those self-defeating beliefs into a positive statement about yourself. Once more, find some evidence to support these statements

Here are some examples:

Self-defeating beliefs	Positive self-beliefs
I'm no good at sport.	I don't shine in team sports but I enjoy non-competitive activities like cycling and dancing.
I'm so unattractive.	I'm unique and I can make the most of what I have.
No one listens to me.	I find communication difficult but I'm getting better at it.

I give up too easily.	I must identify a goal that really motivates me – and tell myself that I deserve to achieve it.

Most of us have a mixture of self-beliefs, some of which are positive and 'empowering', while others are negative and 'disempowering'. It may be that you have low self-image in terms of the work you do. But you might also see yourself as being good at a hobby. The trick is to replace the negative beliefs that stop you getting where you want to go with positive beliefs that will help you to reach your goals.

Coping with disappointment

'Many of life's failures are people who didn't realise how close to success they were when they gave up.'

Thomas Edison (1879)

No matter how clear your goals are, and how carefully you lay out your plans, there are going to be times when things do not work out as you hope. But if you can think like a successful entrepreneur you will be able to bounce back from any failure or disappointment. It is said that Thomas Edison spent $40,000, and performed 1200 experiments before he succeeded in his ambition to invent a safe and inexpensive electric light bulb. It is simple mathematics really. You create more chances to score a goal if you can learn from experience and keep trying when you have failed.

When you attempt something and it goes wrong, you may feel hurt, angry or just plain embarrassed. Your 'failure' could be anything – getting sacked, being turned down for a job or a contract, making a mistake or speaking out of turn. Unless you apply positive thinking, there is a real danger that you might slip into a slough of despondency, feeling that there is little point in carrying on. But do not be discouraged. Try to turn the failure into success by viewing the incident as a chance to learn.

Of course, it is not wrong to let off a bit of steam. It is quite normal to feel a sense of loss or frustration when disappointment occurs – especially if it was your fault. You may feel angry with yourself for making foolish mistakes. It is important to release these bad feelings so that you can move on. If possible talk about them to a friend or relative or write them down. You may like to do something physical, like swimming or running, to help you work off the negative emotions.

After that, the most important thing to do is to learn from the experience. Be brutally honest with yourself about what really happened. What went wrong? There are many reasons why you may have failed:

- Unrealistic goals
- Factors outside your control
- Making mistakes
- Insufficiently developed skills

Try to analyse the events and the behaviour that led to the failure and what you could have done differently. How can you make sure the same thing does not happen again? If it really was your fault, it is important to take responsibility and not blame others for the problem. Above all remember that you are only a 'failure' if you quit when things go wrong. When things do not work out as you planned, what happens is neither good nor bad, but merely information that will help you improve your plan next time around.

When you put the past behind you, your positive attitude will do much to shape what happens to you from here on in. Tell yourself that accidents happen or that everyone makes mistakes or misses deadlines from time to time. None of this makes you a loser. The trick is to demonstrate (to yourself and others) that you recognise what went wrong and are a better person as a result. It will make all the difference to act confidently and maybe even to see the funny side. The result will be that you will keep going long after others give up.

Many people say (in the light of experience) that the 'failure' was the best thing that ever happened to them. It could be a chance to review your career path or to identify what is standing between you and success. If you think positively you can turn almost every so-called failure to your advantage.

Networking know-how

Although being enterprising is about taking charge of one's own life, the world need not be a cold, friendless place for those who have decided to help themselves. Knowing how to use and expand your personal networks is an important element in your quest to become more enterprising. A network is a group of people who can help you to achieve your goals. Networking means building professional relationships with this group and staying in contact with them.

Research indicates that the people who advance their careers through personal contacts have greater job satisfaction and higher incomes than those who do not. And most people now recognise that one of the keys to being successful as a freelancer or an entrepreneur is to have a strong support network.

Who is in your network?
The great thing about a network is that you already have one, consisting of your:

- Relatives and friends
- Bank manager, solicitor and doctor
- Boss, co-workers and business contacts

These people can help you in a variety of ways. They can tell you about job opportunities, they can give you information about skills and courses, they can provide you with inside information about the industry you work in or they can simply provide you with support to help you progress. The way it works is that each person in your network has at least as many contacts as you, so you may have access to all kinds of different people without realising it. Try making a list of the people in your network and then consider what they can do for you. Do not forget that the internet is a fertile source of opportunities for networking.

Summary

Today you have been looking at what it means to be enterprising. You have seen that it all starts with you – how you regard yourself and what you believe you can do. Achieving what you want is only possible if you can think positively, confront your fears and cope with disappointment. It is also important to obtain greater access to ideas and business opportunities by making the extension of your support network a priority.

Work from the heart

We were all born with unique gifts and talents, but the trouble is that few of us know how to find out what they are and to make the most of them. The result is that too many of us drift into unsuitable careers and end up feeling dissatisfied and unfulfilled. The good news is that it is never too late to go back to the drawing board and identify the right kind of work.

Select your employer

It is easy to forget that finding a job is actually a two-way transaction and that you do not have to accept the first offer which comes along. To put yourself in the most powerful position you need to analyse:

- *Yourself:* what are your values and your interests? What experience do you have? What skills and personal qualities can you offer an employer?

- *Your job requirements:* what industries do you want to work in? What role do you want to perform? What working conditions are you looking for? How much money do you want to earn?

Once you have this information, you will be able to evaluate the suitability of various options or opportunities. It may be that your ideal work is not a job at all but a business enterprise or a 'portfolio' of part-time positions. It is not rocket science, but the more information you have the better your decision will be.

Your achievements

Most people undervalue their skills and strengths and this means that they undersell themselves when they are applying for jobs or promotion. The trouble is that we are often embarrassed about mentioning our strong points and feel uncomfortable when others praise us.

For some of us it is self-esteem that blocks our career choice or our career development. Unfortunately, our view of ourselves is often a product of other people's inability to encourage us and show appreciation for the things we do well. Why is it that in many work environments there seems to be a belief that you should just know how well you are doing or that you simply do not need to know!

> 'Sometimes I can't seem to do anything right. My boss criticises me all the time and I get so nervous I'm always making mistakes. I just feel really hopeless – as if I will never achieve anything in my life.'
>
> Eva, marketing consultant

Luckily, you do not have to wait for someone else to value the things that you do and to notice your many talents. You can be your own best friend, your biggest fan, your most reliable source of support. Doing this is not an indulgence. If you do not appreciate what you have to offer, no one else will either!

One way to boost your morale is to think about the things that you like about yourself, the things you are proud of and the things you enjoy doing. These may have nothing to do with work – your tennis-playing ability, for example, the time you went to a party on your own, your sense of humour or your knowledge of the Coen Brothers' films. Again, force yourself to write down at least six things. If you find this hard try writing six sentences that begin 'I feel good about myself when . . .' or 'I like the fact that I . . .'.

Blowing your own trumpet will make you feel really positive about yourself and it may help you to identify some important themes and directions for the future.

Don't be shy – no one is looking over your shoulder!

Your values

These people are all talking about their work values:

> *'Job satisfaction is important to me.'*
>
> *'I don't want to work long hours.'*
>
> *'I enjoy learning new things.'*

Your personal work values are the beliefs and feelings that are important to you; they are central to the quality of your life. The more you are able to pursue a career which allows you to live out your values, the more satisfying your life will be.

By clarifying our values, we may be able to find better ways of realising them both in our jobs and in our lives outside work. There are no rights or wrongs here because everyone has different values.

Your values could be things like:

- Job security
- Good working conditions
- Opportunities for learning new skills
- The expectation of promotion and advancement
- Earning enough to live well
- Achieving something worthwhile
- Having personal power and influence
- Fulfilling my potential
- A sense of belonging
- Doing work that involves a physical effort

Use this list to trigger your thoughts and to help you decide what your personal values are. Make lists of the values that are the most important and the ones that are least important to you.

Then look at your job:

- Are there any values which you have identified as being important to you which do not find expression in the work you do now?
- Do any of your 'least important' values feature in what you do now?
- Can you think of any job or career that would satisfy the values you have identified?

Your interests

> 'Everyone I have ever met who had the courage to do
> what they really wanted, believed in hindsight they had
> made the right decision, regardless of success or
> failure.'
>
> Simon Woodruffe, entrepreneur

The more interested you are in something, the easier it is to
work at it. It can be something very specific like gardening or
using the computer. Or it could be a general interest like
'working with children'. Making a life change demands
determination and hard work, but you can do that if you
really love what you are involved in. It therefore makes sense
to look for work which satisfies your deepest interests, what
you really like doing and what you want to do.

- Make a list of the ten things you most like to do.
- If you could choose to do anything today, what would
  it be?
- Is there anything you would work at for no wage?
- What would you do if you had a guarantee that
  whatever you did, it would succeed?

Once again the answers to these questions will provide you
with clues that may highlight the decisions you need to
make. Leave no stone unturned in your quest for your dream
job. Often the answers to your questions and problems are
closer than you think.

Your skills

We tend to think of ourselves as only having the same potential and abilities as when we left school. We do not take time to take stock of all the things we have learnt and done since then. You will be surprised once you start to do this analysis at the variety of valuable skills that you possess.

Take a piece of paper and draw a line down the centre. On the left list all the jobs you have had, leaving plenty of space between each one. Then on the right note the main responsibilities and skills associated with the job.

Here is an example of one completed by Helen, a sales executive.

Job	Tasks and skills
Shop assistant	Dealing with the public. Handling money/giving change. Checking stock.
Pensions administrator	Answering the telephone. Checking forms. Keeping records. Dealing with figures/calculations. Handling enquiries. Writing letters. Applying policies and rules.
Marketing executive	Dealing with customers. Advertising and promoting products. Telephone skills. Negotiating. Verbal communication. Keeping records. Calculating invoices/sales.

It is important to have a full picture of all the jobs you have had and all the things you have done in them. You may consider some previous jobs as being 'low level' or unimportant and yet you may have done things in them which you can build on in the future. There may be something in one of your jobs that you particularly enjoyed doing which needs to be taken into account in your future plans.

Skills from other life roles

We do not tend to value the things we have learnt through experiences outside work. But you have most certainly added to your stock of skills and abilities by, for example, being a parent, running a home, membership of a sports team or volunteer work.

Take another piece of paper and make a list of your 'life roles' and the skills you use or have used in these roles.

Here is Helen's list as an example.

Life roles	Skills developed or used
Traveller	Language/communication skills. Organising self and others. Planning. Problem solving. Time management.
Captain of hockey team	Cooperating with others. Providing clear direction and leadership. Taking tough or unpopular decisions. Thinking on my feet. Giving feedback.
Parent	Planning. Coordinating more than one task at a time. Making arrangements. Supporting people. Resolving disagreements. Dealing with crises.

You should now have an idea of the wealth of skills you possess through the work you have done and from other aspects of your life. It is particularly important to be aware of the skills you have gained outside the context of work if you have had any gaps in your career.

Your qualities

It is easy to focus on skills and abilities to the exclusion of personal qualities. Yet things like resilience, adaptability and loyalty are highly prized by employers because they make the difference between average performance and exceptional performance. Both positive and negative experiences can develop these attributes.

It is not enough to say that you have a particular quality – that would be too easy! It is important to provide examples of situations in which you have demonstrated this quality. For example, surviving the breakdown of a relationship can show the ability to cope with failure, increase self-reliance, mean that you are able to face rejection, or develop independence and maturity. Once again, take a piece of paper, note down your personal qualities on one side and examples of situations in which you demonstrated each quality on the other side.

Here is Helen's list:

Personal quality	Example of situation
Sense of humour (can see the funny side of most situations).	Organising team meetings.
Determination (always see a project through to completion).	Company newsletter.
Enthusiasm (highly motivated to succeed).	Project to develop new recruitment system.
Confidence (able to act appropriately in any situation).	Presentation at annual conference.

Your needs

Unless you identify your needs when establishing a career direction, there is a real danger of accepting a job which is wrong for you. If you are already in a job which dissatisfies you, you must avoid jumping out of the frying pan into the fire. Unless you know exactly what to look for, the new role could turn out to be just as inadequate as the old one, but in a different way.

So, it is important to take time out to clarify the things which will satisfy you in your future career. Think about the aspects you like and the reasons for your current frustration. You will end up with a profile of your job needs.

Use these questions to analyse your needs:

- Where do you want to work?
- Which skills do you want to use?
- What sort of atmosphere or environment do you like to work in?
- What salary do you require?
- Who do you want to work with?

Here is Helen's list:

Needs

Maximum half-hour commute.
Modern workplace – clean, quiet, attractive.
Freedom to set own schedule.
Work where high standards are valued.
Minimum salary of £28,000.
Work as a member of a high-performing team.

Jobs which do not match all of your needs may not be completely unsuitable. There may be other factors which compensate for the missing items. It is still important to set your criteria as a starting point for making your selection.

Unless you make a conscious decision to get into the driving seat, you run the risk of letting your life just drift, or of allowing other people to control the important decisions you should be making for yourself. By identifying the kind of work you would love to do, you will invest more passionately in your job and become a more valuable employee.

Summary

Today you have been looking at ways of pinpointing the kind of career or the type of work that may be right for you. First you tried out lifelining which allows you to take stock of the way that things have happened to you in the past. After that you listed your achievements and identified your values, interests, skills and qualities. With that lot under your belt you can hardly fail! But you will not be able to satisfy your career needs unless you can adapt quickly to make the most of new opportunities. See tomorrow's chapter for tips on becoming more flexible

Learn to love change

In the past few years, most companies have undergone extensive changes. Everywhere you look there is a bewildering flurry of management buzz-words. Everyone seems to be downsizing, re-engineering, merging, refocusing, reorganising or restructuring. The fact that nothing stays the same for very long can be very disturbing and stressful for those on the receiving end. But it is not the organisation's fault. Often its very survival depends on how effectively it can respond to changes in the business environment. It cannot afford to stand still because, if it does, the competition will race ahead. Similarly, if you want to develop your career, it is vital to learn to expect change. Get used to the idea that change is happening around you all the time, so you can make the most of the new opportunities that come with it.

Change is not what it used to be

Change is an essential part of being human. If this were not the case we would still be riding around on horseback, or using pigeons to send messages. What is different in the early years of the 21st century is not so much what has changed, but the pace of change.

In the space of a couple of decades we have seen dramatic changes in the world at large, in our own communities and in our individual lives. Much of the change we see around us springs from the rapid evolution of technology and the increasing speed with which new developments become practical realities. The stuff of yesterday's science fiction –

instant communication, talking cars, armchair banking, a TV on your wrist – is suddenly today's reality. New technology changes both people's expectations and the economic facts that determine what is produced and at what price, where it is made and who buys it.

You must expect to change jobs frequently and to make at least one significant change of direction during your working life. You may have to get used to more flexible ways of working, for instance payment for results rather than your time, short-term contracts, self-employment, a portfolio career.

Your attitude to change

Change is here to stay, whether we like it or not. We are foolish if we get angry about it or try to ignore its signs. Successful people use change for their own ends, instead of only reacting to it. Change, looked at positively, can in most cases be another word for development or growth – we can

all participate in it productively, enjoy it and profit from it –
if we choose to.

Your reaction will depend on how important the change is
and whether there are personal implications for you. Think of
a major change which has happened to you at work. Did you
simply go along with it without thinking of the impact on
your job and on your career? Did you get upset, fight against
the change, refuse to cooperate? Or did you try to get used to
it quickly and go out of your way to make it work?

Admittedly there will be some changes that you simply
cannot stomach. The third take-over in as many years. Yet
another boss fresh from an MBA course with brilliant ideas
for improving productivity. The company is relocating to
premises 150 km away. If you cannot influence what is
happening and commit to the change, it could be time to get
out of there. No one can blame you for wanting to leave an
organisation and a job which no longer meet your needs. Do
not waste energy agonising about loyalty – the organisation
will not thank you for staying around if you are unhappy in
your job. In the end, it is best for both you and your
employer if you move on as quickly as possible.

How do you handle change?

Do this quiz for a quick insight into how you handle change
at the moment.

> **1** You work for a local authority. Your boss tells you
> that a new appraisal system will go live next month.
> This will affect both how you work and how much
> you are paid. What do you say?

   A 'What's an appraisal system?'
   B 'I guess I'll have to put up with it.'
   C 'I'd better find out more about this.'
   D 'I'm ready for my first appraisal, are you?'

2 You need a job and a new company is moving into your area soon. What do you do?

   A Nothing – you know nothing about it because you do not keep up with local news.
   B Wait to see if they advertise for someone with your skills and experience.
   C Phone up and find that the jobs were all advertised and filled weeks ago.
   D Contact the Human Resources department immediately to find out what sort of skills the company is looking for. Then decide how you can best present yourself as just the person they need.

3 You find out that a firm of consultants has advised your company to shut down the IT department and to outsource all the functions that you and your colleagues currently perform. What do you do?

   A Feel bewildered because you did not realise what was about to happen.
   B Complain loudly because you are going to lose your job.
   C Start looking around for jobs in other departments and in other companies.
   D When the news was announced you had already put a business plan together and acquired sufficient finance to set up a small business,

selling IT services both to your current employer and others.

4 Recently some long-standing customers have been complaining about late deliveries. They are threatening to defect to a new competitor. Do you:

A Wonder why there are suddenly so many complaints – you were not aware that there were any problems.

B Feel confident that the manager will step in and sort things out sooner or later.

C Stand back and watch things go from bad to worse, but it is none of your business so you say nothing.

D Approach your manager with a few ideas of your own on how you can improve things and fight off the threat from the competitor.

If you ticked mainly **As**, you are the sort of person who rarely sees what is going on until it affects you directly. It is therefore easy for change to threaten you because it sneaks up on you, and you are not prepared for it. You probably feel negative about the idea of change in general, preferring the status quo and resenting it when it happens.

If you ticked mainly **Bs**, you have probably gone through life expecting things to continue in much the same way as they always did. For you change has always meant more of the same. When unexpected changes have taken place you have tended to wait to see what happens rather than try to exert influence or plan your response. You will take advantage of an opportunity if it comes along and hits you on the head. But you tend not to dig beneath the surface or look at problems from another angle in order to come up with a solution.

If you ticked mainly **Cs**, you are well aware of the changes that are going on around you and are affecting the way you live. You may even study these changes, discuss them with friends, complain about them. But you feel unable to influence what is happening in any way. You say 'It doesn't matter what we think, they will do whatever they want in the end' or 'It's my bad luck – these things always happen to me'. You feel like a victim, powerless in the face of forces that are out of your control.

If you ticked mainly **Ds**, you have a very positive attitude to change. You are aware of what changes are in the air and their implications for you. If you need information or help you know where to get it. When it seems as though change will be for the worse you do not accept it lying down, but, on the other hand, you probably do not waste effort fighting the inevitable.

Tips for managing change

By understanding that you do not have to be a passive onlooker, you can enjoy more of the opportunities change can provide and suffer less from its threats. Here is a list of eight principles which should guide your behaviour in coping with change:

1 *Be open to change*: avoid any temptation to be defensive and to hold on to what you may lose as a result of the change; instead look at the positive things that you will gain in exchange.

2 *Deal with the here and now*: do not be too obsessed with how

things were before, or with how they might turn out in the future. Make sure that you handle the tasks that you face at the moment.

3 *Be positive and active*: do not be content to react to things passively; be prepared to make things happen.

4 *Harness your feelings*: managing change is an emotional business as well as a rational one. Be prepared to use your feelings, and the energy that comes from them, to positive effect.

5 *Be realistic*: there is a real danger when coping with change that you may deal in fantasy rather than reality: fantasies about how things are likely to turn out and fantasies about how they were before. Keep your feet on the ground and deal with the facts, positive as well as negative.

6 *Avoid tunnel vision*: there is always more than one way to get to where you want to be. Make the effort to look for the alternatives even if they are hard to find at first.

7 *Develop your skills*: prepare for change by taking personal responsibility for keeping your skills and knowledge up to date.

8 *Like yourself*: the key to successful change management is self-esteem. Pay attention to your positive qualities and realise that you really do have a great deal to offer.

Many of these skills and approaches will be valuable to you, not only as you prepare yourself for personal change, but also if you decide to move up the career ladder into management. In fact, change management can be seen as the most important part of anybody's work.

Looking after yourself

The emotions that you go through when making a change, no matter how positive the end result, will always be mixed. If you feel threatened by the change you may suffer from a whole gamut of emotions – shock, denial, grief, anger and depression. Any significant development in your life, either positive or negative, brings with it new stresses and potential pitfalls as well as new opportunities.

The key to understanding the process is recognising that any change involves some 'loss'. You will give up some aspect of your present situation which has become an important part of your life.

But change is never total. It is very easy to lose sight of the fact that even if you are thinking about making major changes to your life, a great deal will stay the same. This is an important point. When we go through the process of change

we need areas of life that we can hang on to. We can all cope with an enormous amount of change, pressure, complexity and confusion – as long as we can be confident that there are still areas that will stay relatively stable. Identifying these 'stability zones' in advance is an important way of preparing for change.

Your stability zone could be: ideas, like a strong commitment to a religious belief; places, like your home or the town you grew up in; things, like a family heirloom; people, like the members of your family or long-standing friends; or organisations, like a club or society that you belong to.

These areas of your life will give you comfort and support. They have helped you to cope with change in the past and they will do so again.

Summary

Today we have seen the importance of being in control of your career when everything is in perpetual motion around you. It is no good complaining or getting angry when the organisation shifts in response to the forces that surround it. That kind of attitude will only do you harm in the end. The problem is that, no matter how you feel about changes, they are still going to occur. The question is how you can make sure that what is happening works to your advantage, rather than against you.

Stay in school

Today's habit is all about lifelong learning – because the only way to remain competitive in the job market is to invest in your own growth. If you are lucky your employer will help out with this, but ultimately the responsibility is entirely your own.

For some, staying in school will mean signing on for an MBA, a degree or a diploma in a particular area. But sometimes it only takes a short course or a certain kind of experience to acquire the skills you need to enhance your market value.

Be a lifelong learner

The world is changing fast and it will not take long for your skills to become outdated. Advancing technology and the rising flood of information make it hard to keep up with what is going on. Even new graduates can be left behind in just a few years. If you are a technical wizard you cannot sit back for long because new products and new techniques are

being developed all the time. And some jobs do not even have time to change – they simply fade away.

These days, standing still is not an option for anyone who wants to grow their career. It is not only advancing technology that influences what you need to know. Developments in the national and international economy and social and political trends all make an enormous difference to the way in which you carry out your work. The world is moving on and if you do not shift with it, you will be left high and dry on the beach when the tide goes out.

What do you need to learn?

You might be looking for a course with a specific job or promotion in mind. Or perhaps you feel out of date with what is going on in your chosen field. No matter how old you are or whether you have any qualifications, there is a suitable option for you.

For training to be effective, you must first know in some detail what specific knowledge and skills the job involves, what you already possess and what gaps the learning or development can fill. This assessment will result in an identification of:

- How you measure up to the required performance standard
- What learning or development you need to fill the gaps or to develop your potential

Analysing your job

The first step in deciding which skills you need to learn, is to work out which skills you need to do your job effectively. If you are not in a job or you are aiming for promotion, look at the skills required for the job you would like to do. This is not as difficult as it may seem. Start with your job description if you have one. Think about the things that you do every day or the things that you would do in the job you are aiming for.

You need to consider the core skills of the job, the basic behaviours that apply to any type of work (things like communication, team work and managing time) and any specialist or technical skills which you need to do the job effectively (things like vehicle maintenance, catering, using computer applications or managing finance).

You may also want to find out if a National Vocational Qualification (NVQ) has been published for all or part of your job role. If so, this will help considerably in your task of analysing job skills and knowledge. NVQs break down occupations into:

- Units of competence – the main task area
- Elements of competence – the smaller task areas

You can contact the relevant National Training Organisation (NTO) for details of the NVQ that may be right for you.

NVQs are awarded at Levels 1 to 5, covering everything from basic to professional level skills. If you use the NVQ standards to analyse your learning needs, you may also decide to enrol on a suitable NVQ programme and work towards the relevant qualification. You can check if specific

courses are available by contacting your professional
association or your local Learning and Skills Council.

Analysing yourself
Once you know which skills you need for your current or
future job, the next step is to analyse the extent to which you
have those skills. To do this you will need to reflect on your
own performance and identify particular areas of difficulty.
This may be easier said than done. For one thing there is a
danger in over or underestimating your capabilities. Try to
be as honest as possible. It is always a good idea to balance
your subjective ideas with the opinions of your boss and/or
colleagues. It is also dangerous to assume that your skills are
developed to the same level across all the areas you are
considering. Use an analysis sheet like the one below to help
you recognise these differences.

Skills required	Good at this	Need to work on this	Complete beginner
Managing others			
Budget planning			
Presentation skills			
Report writing			
Project management			

Two or three priorities for learning should come out of this
analysis. These could be things you need to learn for your

current job or things that will support your career
development or job applications.

How are you going to learn?

When people think of learning or development, formal
training is often what first comes to mind. However, it is
important to remember that learning is not something that
just happens in the classroom. In fact, we all acquire skills
and knowledge in a variety of ways both at work and in
every part of our lives.

Where did you learn most of your:	At school/ university	On a course	At work	Other (specify)
Technical skills?				
Technical knowledge?				
Interpersonal skills (working with others etc)?				
Ability to manage/ organise?				
Ability to calculate/ manage budgets?				
Ability to manage yourself and your time?				

You may have discovered that you acquired many of your skills and much of your knowledge while you were actually doing a job. People continually acquire new skills, knowledge and attitudes without any formal process of training taking place. Here are some of the commonly-used methods which can be easily arranged at work.

- Job rotation
- 'In at the deep end'
- Shadowing an experienced person
- Discussion groups
- Reading
- Guided practice
- Covering for holidays
- Working in a team
- Talking to a manager or mentor
- Attending exhibitions, conferences or seminars
- Watching videos or TV programmes
- Analysing mistakes
- Working on a special project or assignment

Some of the methods on the list are simple and inexpensive, while others are more sophisticated and require a lot of preparation and administration. It is important that the methods you select take account of what you want to learn, the time and money you have available and how you prefer to learn.

Doing a course
There will be occasions when you will need to seek a more formal course to fit your requirements. Your organisation may offer a number of in-house courses but if there is

nothing suitable you can look at what colleges and private providers are offering. The market place is saturated with providers. You might consider:

- Local colleges
- Polytechnics
- Business Schools
- Commercial training organisations
- Government-sponsored schemes
- Professional institutions
- National examining bodies
- Employers' federations
- Trade Union facilities
- Online courses
- Open learning courses
- Correspondence courses

The course you choose will depend on a number of factors including suitability of the subject matter, personal preference, finances and time available. If you are not sure which course to take, you may be able to get advice from a careers counsellor, your boss or your Human Resources (HR) Department.

Learning successfully

You only have to watch small children interacting with the world around them to confirm that human beings are born to learn. In fact we all derive a great deal of satisfaction and pleasure from learning successfully. Remember feeling elated the day you finally passed your driving test? Then there was the quiet sense of contentment when you made a perfectly smooth cheese sauce. Why is it, then, that many of us find the idea of learning so daunting? Why do we give up so easily? The answer is that we cannot and will not learn successfully unless we have a good reason to learn, we have support from others and we can see that we are making progress.

Finding support

Although we have stressed your personal responsibility for planning and achieving your learning objectives, this does not mean that you have to isolate yourself from colleagues and friends who can offer moral support or practical help. Most people now realise that it is crucial to have a strong support network to make it as an independent learner. Networking means building and using a wide-ranging list of people who can assist you in a variety of ways:

- Your contacts can provide you with opportunities to learn or experience something new
- There may be people who can talk things over with you and help you to overcome problems
- Your network may be a source of feedback that you have never tapped into before

Some organisations encourage mentoring to help people learn and develop, but if no such system is available there is nothing to stop you from taking the initiative and finding a mentor for yourself. A mentor is a manager, friend or colleague who agrees to help you to develop your career by supporting and advising you. The most important point is that your mentor must be someone you can talk to easily and someone you can trust. You might even decide to have more than one mentor – one to give you encouragement in a general way and others to help you learn particular job skills.

Keeping a learning log
Keeping a learning log or diary is a good way of recording your progress towards achieving your goal. It is motivating because it helps you to measure how far you have come – rather than focusing on how far you still have to travel. A learning log will help you to remember what you have learned and keep you committed to your programme.

Here is an example:

What I did	What I learned	How I can apply this in future

Your log will help you to maintain an accurate record of your achievements and it will be a powerful stimulus for your future learning. You will begin to see how different kinds of learning experiences are moving you closer to where you want to be. In time, you will find that writing up your experiences can be quite therapeutic. Many seasoned 'loggers' get a real buzz from getting things out of their system and into a diary or onto a computer.

Managing your time
It is important to give yourself time targets for study because doing so will help to motivate you and keep you focused on your study goals. Decide on some completion dates for each chunk of work and draw up a timetable or note the key dates in your diary. Do not let things fester if you become demoralised – discuss any problems with your tutor or manager.

It is a good idea to set aside a certain amount of time each week for studying and mark these periods in your diary. Tuck in the hours where you have them available, make use of bus rides or train journeys and try to schedule your studies in the times when you know that you can concentrate.

Building a portfolio
Creating a career portfolio is another way of reminding yourself about your progress and making sure you do not give up. This is simply a scrapbook or file that contains evidence of your achievements. 'Evidence' can be anything that demonstrates what you are capable of: copies of reports, certificates, photos, articles in newsletters, action plans, diary notes, letters. The list is endless. Do not just collect the

evidence – consider what each item says about you and your skills. An e-mail from a satisfied customer may be evidence of your customer service skills, a report could be evidence of your ability to organise and present information, a diary page might be evidence of your time-management skills.

The evidence you collect could be useful in a variety of situations: during a performance appraisal; when negotiating a salary increase; or when applying for a new job. The best thing is that your portfolio will help you to keep a positive attitude about yourself because it highlights your skills and achievements rather than the things which cause problems.

The right place to study
Most successful students have one place where all they do is study. It may be a home office, a corner of the bedroom or a cubby hole under the stairs. Your special place should be somewhere you want to go to, not a punishment area or a prison cell! This will get you in the mood for studying and help you to concentrate. Consider adding special touches like colourful pictures, fresh flowers and a perfume oil burner. These will stimulate your senses and make you more receptive to the things you are studying.

Stay positive
If you are like most people, studying does not come easily. The very word is associated with negative things like 'drudgery', 'burden' and 'bore'. No matter what your experience of school or college in the past, it is important to develop a positive attitude towards studying.

Tell yourself several times every day 'I am making good progress' and 'I am going to succeed'. Think about the benefits you hope to gain from completing what you have started. Set yourself inspiring goals and promise yourself some form of reward or treat when you have achieved them.

It also helps to find new and interesting ways to approach subjects which have bored you in the past. If you throw yourself into your work with enthusiasm, learning will soon cease to be such a chore. You will soon begin to make progress, and your success will give you energy and optimism for further study.

Summary

Wednesday has been a brief tour round the things you have to do to be a 'lifelong learner'. Well, no one said that having a successful career was going to be easy, did they? Because you cannot depend on your organisation to give you the skills you need to be successful, you have to do it for yourself. You start by identifying what you need to learn, then you decide how you are going to learn and finally you simply go ahead and do it! It is a good idea to find people to support you and keep a learning log or diary so that you can literally watch your skills grow. You will need lots of motivation to make this work, and we discuss more about this important topic tomorrow.

Manage your own motivation

Motivation matters because if you've got it you can achieve whatever you want in life. Without it you may be unsure of where you are heading or how you should be spending your time. But you cannot wait for someone else to encourage you to give your best; to move your career forward it is crucial to get into the habit of managing your own motivation.

What motivates you?

Whenever you have achieved things in your life, you were probably motivated by:

- *External factors*: things outside you, like the carrot and the stick.
- *Internal factors*: things that come from inside you, like wanting to prove yourself, looking for a challenge or simply needing to keep busy.

The important point is that no one else can motivate a donkey, a zebra or a king penguin for that matter. Motivation is an internal drive – these animals will only move if they feel sufficiently motivated. It is the same for human beings; we have to find a good reason for doing things, a purpose which will inspire us and keep us on track during the tough times. If you work in an enlightened organisation, you may get help with this. The management team will arrange things and provide a vision, set goals and identify objectives which you can buy into so that you will feel motivated. Otherwise you are on your own.

In the end it is better to find your own motivation because this stretches you and makes the most of your potential. If you can identify what motivates you, you will be a more valuable employee and your career will benefit as a result. If you can find out about your most important motivating factors, you will be able to use this information to empower yourself.

In reality, most people are moved by a combination of internal and external factors. This is valuable because the greater the motivation, the more effective people are in what they do. Think about your own experience for a moment. Make a list of two or three things that motivated you to achieve something that you found complex and difficult.

The items on your list may fit into one or more of the following categories:

- Achievement
- Approval
- Curiosity
- Acquisitiveness

Try to turn any negative factors around and express them in a positive way. For example, if you wrote 'fear of failure', the motivation could be 'achievement'. If you wrote 'anxiety about money', the motivation could be 'acquisitiveness'. It is true that factors like pain and fear are powerful motivators, but it is much better to be travelling towards something inspiring than running away from something unpleasant!

These motivating factors rarely act in isolation. You could be motivated by achievement, the desire for approval and acquisitiveness all at the same time.

- If you are motivated by the need to achieve, you must make sure that you are aware of success when it happens. This means monitoring your progress, tracking it, charting it. Small easily achievable steps are more motivating than ambitious aims that take a long time to achieve
- If you are motivated by the need to gain others' approval, you will find it useful to develop a support network which will give you encouragement and make you feel valued. If your organisation does not provide you with sufficient support, you can probably get what you need from other sources, both face to face, over the telephone and online. It may also help you to seek feedback from your boss or your clients
- If you are motivated by curiosity, you could get involved in projects and assignments which nurture your interests and your desire to find things out for yourself. People who are motivated by curiosity often enjoy interviewing customers, researching new developments or joining project teams

- If you are motivated by acquisitiveness, your goals need to focus on getting a better job, a higher salary and other material rewards

Once you have pinpointed the things that motivate you, the next step is to use these to drive you to get from where you are to where you want to go. Easier said than done, perhaps, but again you can use some management tools to clarify your direction and keep yourself on track.

Get the picture

To maintain your motivation, it is important to set some specific and tangible goals that correspond with the things that motivate you. Unfortunately, it can sometimes be very difficult to think of anything you would like to do. Although the ideas are not in your conscious mind, they may be in your subconscious mind if you can find a way of reaching them.

The trick is to create a clear mental picture of what it is you want to achieve. Do not worry if your ideas seem ambitious, it is important to avoid limiting yourself at this early stage. If you want a new career, imagine yourself being there. If you want to be accepted on a course, imagine what it would be like to study that subject. Picture yourself being and doing whatever you want to achieve in your career.

Make the image as stimulating and interesting as possible by including colours, sounds, textures and scents. Make it three-dimensional so you can step inside and feel what it is like to achieve the success you desire. Where are you? What are you doing and saying? How are others reacting to you? Feel calm, comfortable, courageous and confident.

Visualisation works best if you are relaxed, so you need to find at least ten minutes when you can sit or lie comfortably without being disturbed. Once you are relaxed, you can start to put your imagination to work; you will be amazed at the variety and quality of images and feelings your brain can conjure up if you let go. It is best to replay the visualisation several times to make a real difference to how motivated you feel. The more often you run it, the easier it is to bring it back and each time you will enjoy the experience more and feel more determined to succeed.

This is probably the most powerful technique you can use to get what you want in life. It is used by sports people, politicians, entertainers and self-made millionaires all over the world. How do you think they learned to believe in themselves and to be so confident? Many of them have no more natural talent than you or I – the difference is that they drive themselves on towards clear goals and they are never put off by mistakes or failure.

Set some goals

To achieve your visualisation, you need to translate it into concrete goals. This is where realism raises its ugly head because there is no point in setting yourself up to fail. Make a note of your goal and check that it is SMART:

- *Specific*: stating clearly what you intend to achieve will help you work out exactly what you have to do to achieve it.
- *Measurable*: how will you know when you have achieved your goal? What will be different? What would other people notice or say about you?
- *Active*: try to frame your goal in terms of actions, rather than things you will have or things that will happen to you. It is a matter of being in control. So do not say 'to get my boss's job' because he or she may not be intending to leave. Say instead 'to develop my management skills, gain experience of working at a higher level and to apply for promotion'.
- *Realistic*: are you prepared to accept the costs involved in

achieving the goal? For instance, although in theory it might be possible for you to become a vet, it could be unrealistic to dedicate many years of your life to full-time study.

• *Timebound*: giving yourself a deadline will help to eliminate procrastination. Your plan should show what you have to do between now and the deadline to achieve your goal. Do not make the timescale too ambitious – always allow time for unexpected events.

Make a plan

'I am in the fourth year of my Ph.D., supposedly at the 'writing-up' stage, but am having trouble doing any writing! My usual tendency towards procrastination has reached epic proportions. In truth, I haven't done anything on it for months although I worry about it constantly. How can I motivate myself to complete the damn thing?'

Eva, marketing consultant

Your plan is like a route map that you draw up at the start of a journey, it is useful to have one but you do not have to follow it slavishly. The plan will:

• Break down a challenging goal into achievable steps
• Specify a timeframe for achieving each step
• Identify who you need to contact for information and support

Do not forget to take account of your own resources, such as your own personal qualities like determination or your skills. This is important because sometimes we do not put enough value on our strengths when faced with a challenge.

Finally, try to anticipate how the plan could be sabotaged. What things do you tend to do to stop yourself getting what you want and deserve? Your plan will not work if you always put others' needs before your own or if you are easily demoralised or distracted. How could other people sabotage you by their attitudes or action? There may be many powerful influences which you need to recognise and neutralise.

Here is an example of a plan, made by Jan who is a marketing officer.

Goal	Within 12 months I want to achieve a £4000 increase in salary, doing a job which involves operating a budget and supervising others
Action	Clarify the kind of job I want Check the market Find out about suitable opportunities (internet, newspapers, journals) Make appropriate contacts Prepare a new CV Develop my skills
Resources	Online information about the job market Skills gained through my jobs Good organiser Work done so far on CV Books and professional journals

	Good references from previous employers
	Newspapers/job info on net
Support	Colleagues Sue, Charlie
	My partner David
	My mentor Joanna
Sabotage	Myself – getting too tired/not making the time
	Fear of rejection
	Wanting applications to be too perfect so not starting or finishing them
	David thinks a higher level job would be too pressurised
	Intense competition for higher level jobs
Action to counter sabotage	Early nights
	Healthy self-talk
	Time/stress management
	Talk to David – be assertive do not argue

Review your plan and check that it is still working in the way that was intended. You should always be prepared to change it if unforeseen circumstances arise.

Reward yourself

Implementing your plan may not be easy. You may have to be prepared to accept a new challenge, to push yourself harder or even to make a journey into unknown territory. One strategy for preventing yourself from falling by the wayside is to promise yourself some exciting rewards for your progress and achievements. Nothing has changed really since the days when our parents promised a packet of crisps if we could swim a length of the pool. Rewards are great incentives and morale boosters – it is human nature.

The rewards you give yourself can be big or small, tangible or intangible. But they must be something that you would really appreciate, for example:

- A long soak in the tub when you have been studying hard for an exam
- A night out with friends when you have finished preparing your CV
- A new shirt or a pair of shoes when you have landed an important interview
- A weekend away when you have successfully completed an important project

Receiving feedback

Do not forget to obtain rewards in the form of praise and appreciation from others. This is vital for your motivation and morale, especially in a performance review or after a job interview. You must not be too modest to ask for feedback and/or praise if it is not forthcoming. If someone praises you, try not to be dismissive, embarrassed or suspicious. Accept it in good spirit as you would a gift.

People are often very poor at giving feedback, so you may have to take charge of the situation in order to get the information you need. Here is what to do if someone gives you negative feedback or criticism.

- *Do not be defensive or self-justifying*: the person giving the feedback will almost certainly have good reasons for drawing attention to areas you need to work on.
- *Clarify what is being said*: check that you have understood by repeating, summarising or asking questions.
- *Ask for evidence*: ask for examples of the behaviour or performance in question. This will help you to understand what it is that the person does or does not find acceptable.
- *Give your side of the story*: state your case or explain mitigating circumstances, but stick to the facts and do not try to blame other people.
- *Agree what needs to be done*: ask the other person to suggest ways in which you might improve the situation. Decide what you are going to do to correct any problems.

Feedback, praise and other tangible rewards will help you appreciate that you are making progress and encourage you to keep moving on towards your goal. They will also make you more aware of your own value. The stronger you feel, the more confident you will be when looking for jobs, courses of study or other opportunities. If you experience rejection you will not be demolished, and your belief in yourself will help you to survive hurt and disappointment.

Summary

Today the focus has been on motivation, which is a vital ingredient of a successful career. Only the lucky few have managers who understand the need to build the structures and develop a culture in which people feel motivated. For most of us motivation is something we have to do for ourselves. This means identifying goals to inspire us and planning strategies to achieve them. It is also important to measure our progress and achievements in terms of rewards and feedback.

Start here and now

One thing we learn as we get older is that, whatever we do, time continues to tick away day in and day out. It does not matter we spend it – in a meeting, drafting a report, surfing the internet, staring at the wall – time just carries on passing by. Pretty soon we start to get older and we realise that our limited allocation of time is being used up at a frightening rate. If we are ever going to achieve anything in life we had better start right here, right now.

The activity trap

One reason for poor time management is that managers are often so busy they simply cannot stop and think about whether or not what they are doing is actually getting them anywhere. It is like trying to think about draining the swamp when you are being attacked by alligators. You know it is important to get time management sorted out and you resolve to do something about it, but only when you have the time.

The problem is that if you let things drift, you can fall into the activity trap. This means that your activities – the way you spend your time day in and day out – may actually be standing in the way of getting where you really want to go.

If you are in the activity trap, you may be one of the following kinds of people.

A fire-fighter

You are a fire-fighter if you never have a minute to spare and are always in a panic, dealing with matters which are 'top priority', 'urgent' or 'vital'. The trouble with 'crisis management' is that it is usually very stressful for everyone involved and it makes people cut corners or make mistakes.

A soft touch

You are a soft touch if you are always at everyone else's beck and call, even though you know that you are already under pressure. Unfortunately, taking other people's problems on board means that you have little time to devote to your own priorities. You are also depriving others of opportunities to take responsibility or to make their own decisions.

A donkey

You are like a donkey on a treadmill if you are trapped into a dull pattern of doing the same things day after day or week after week. Your life may be easy but your activities are unchallenging. You may well feel frustrated because you are in a rut, never getting anywhere.

A dabbler

You are a dabbler if you move from one activity to the next, always looking for satisfaction but never actually finding it. The problem with dabbling is that you never focus your efforts on mastering a single area of your life.

A tornado

Do you travel through life at 90 miles an hour, packing every day with wall-to-wall activities, never pausing to catch your breath? The difficulty here is that you are probably putting both yourself and anyone around you under great stress even though you do not realise it. You may be afraid to stop for a moment because, if you do, you will have to consider where it is all taking you in the end.

Avoiding the activity trap

The only way out of the activity trap is to focus on what you really want to achieve, to identify your priorities and only then to decide on how to use your time to best advantage.

Where does the time go?

Very few people have a true picture of how they spend their time. Many of us think we know, but in reality our memory of what we have done and for how long we did it is usually wildly inaccurate. Without a reasonable idea of where your time is going, it is hard to see where you can make changes and improvements.

The best way to find out what happens to your valuable time is to keep a log for a week. Note what you did each day and how long each activity lasted. Many people think this is going to be very tedious, so they never actually get round to doing it. This is a pity because without one it is hard to be realistic about how you spend your time and anyway it is not nearly so boring once you have made a start.

If you find it hard to remember how you spent your time, try recording your notes at intervals during the day, rather than every two or three days or at the end of the week. Once you have kept a time log for a few days, think about where your time went, and what you want to do to change things.

For example:

- If you only spent a short time on a project or activity that is really important for you, you may like to look at ways of increasing this
- If you wasted a lot of time on routine or unimportant activities, plan how you can cut this down
- If you logged a lot of interruptions, consider how you can reduce these
- If you carried out very few of the tasks you planned to do on a particular day, consider ways of making sure that those things get done

Your priorities

You cannot manage your time effectively unless you know why you want to have time. What do you like doing? What would you like to be doing less of? What are your ambitions and your goals? What is it all for? The aim of time

management is not just to help you become better organised. It is also to make sure that you invest your time in things that benefit you and that move your life forward. Once you know what your priorities are, you can start to manage the demands on your time and devote more of that time to the tasks that are really important for you.

Life balance
Getting your life in balance means investing your time in ways that are important to you. To find out whether or not you are doing what you really want to, you can analyse how you allocate your available time to your main life areas and compare this with how you would like to spend your time. If you keep a time log you will gain the information you need to make this calculation. Otherwise you can make a guess.

Your life areas could be any or all of the following:

Draw a bar chart to show how much time you would like to

- Paid work
- Travel
- Family
- Chores
- Study
- Voluntary work
- Leisure
- Physical exercise
- Sleep

spend on the different areas in a typical week. Do not include all 11 areas, only include the ones that are relevant for you. Then produce another chart which shows how much time you actually spend on each area.

Finally, ask yourself a few questions. Are you investing your time in areas that benefit you, that help you to move your life forward? Or is your life being dictated by others? Do you feel that you spend enough time with your partner or family? Do you make time during the week for physical exercise? The answers to these questions will help you to make some decisions about any changes you want to make.

Your goals
We all have goals, even though we are not always conscious of them. However, we are not going to get far with goals like 'to pay the bills', 'to make ends meet', 'to survive', 'to see what happens', 'to wait for something to come along'. The times when we really move forward are when we have more challenging and inspirational goals in view – 'to pass my driving test', 'to go on holiday', 'to look for a new job', 'to move house' or 'to gain an A level in Spanish'.

If you clarify your goals and focus hard on them, you will find that you begin to realise them almost subconsciously. What happens is that you put yourself in a position to apply your motivation, your resources and your time in achieving what you want.

Your goals can be as generalised or specific as you like, for example:

- To be fitter and healthier (general)
- To clear out the filing cabinet (specific)
- To relax and stay calm in crisis situations (general)
- To become a landscape gardener (specific)
- To cut down on the number of hours I work (general)
- To get a new job by Christmas (specific)
- To improve our after-sales services (general)
- To increase the business turnover by 20 per cent (specific)

Make sure that:

- Your goals are within your personal control. For example, if you want to have your boss's job, your success depends on what another person decides to do – and he or she may stick around much longer than you anticipated!
- You have got what it takes to fulfil your goals. There is no point, for example in deciding at the age of 56 that you would like to become a surgeon or an astronaut. You have to be realistic, without underestimating your potential

Breaking your goals down into manageable chunks is a crucial element of your success. Get into the habit of sitting down once a week (say on a Friday evening or sometime over the weekend) and identifying some steps you can take over the next few days to get closer to your goals. These activities are the 'vital few' priorities which will enable you to achieve what you want. They are the ones which matter most to you, so you need to make sure that you allocate sufficient time to them.

Overcoming procrastination

Do you wish you could actually write that report instead of thinking about it all the time? Do you long to be able to make a start on developing the business into new areas? What about that evening class you always intended to join, the book you wanted to write, the world tour you would love to organise?

Many people procrastinate because they feel that they work best under pressure, putting off the really big jobs until the last possible moment to meet deadlines. Although this approach does succeed sometimes, working under pressure is stressful and may make you cut corners. In addition, more problems will arise as the deadline approaches and everything else goes by the board.

It is important to find the true reasons why you procrastinate, not just the excuses that you make for yourself. It could be that you feel genuinely overwhelmed at the size or the difficulty of the task that faces you or that you are anxious there will not be time to do the job well. It may even be that you are hoping that if you put something off for long enough, someone else will eventually do it!

If you are a procrastinator you must start by admitting (at least to yourself) that you have a problem. You could try:

- Telling yourself firmly what you will gain from doing the task (you will get a real boost from completing tasks that you find difficult or unpleasant)
- Accepting that a task is not going to go away if you procrastinate (the longer you put it off the worse it will get)
- Making up your mind to face up to unpleasant tasks (it will help to think about the times when you have succeeded in completing unpleasant tasks in the past)

Next, you can start to do something about the problem. You may like to try one or more of the following techniques for overcoming procrastination.

- Do the worst job first
- Break a big job down into small tasks
- If getting started is the main problem, do not start at the beginning – begin anywhere. The important thing is to make a start!
- If you have not got a deadline for completion, set your own
- Reward yourself at stages throughout the job and when it is finished
- Set time aside in your diary for doing a job you hate
- Do not allow yourself to stop until you have worked for at least one hour

If you set your mind to it, you will be able to think of other ways of reducing your procrastination. Ask your friends and colleagues what they do about the problem and experiment with the techniques they use. Most people find that procrastination is actually just an unhelpful habit which can be overcome by learning better habits.

Challenging interruptions

Your best laid plans for the day, and ultimately for your entire life, may be thrown into disarray if you allow interruptions to distract you from what you have planned to do.

If you get a lot of phone interruptions at work, try:

- To use an answerphone to 'screen' phone calls and only take the urgent calls. Deal with the low priority calls in batches when you have time
- To ask colleagues to take messages for you when you are working on an important task. Do the same for them when they need some undisturbed time
- To limit the amount of time you spend on incoming phone calls

If other people constantly interrupt you at work, try:

- To tell people who pop in for a chat that you will see them at coffee break or at lunch-time
- To close your door and/or put up a 'do not disturb' notice
- To tell visitors firmly but politely that you are busy and cannot be interrupted
- To set a limit on the amount of time you can spare for an unscheduled meeting
- To cut down social talk and politely ask the person to get to the point
- To discourage unexpected visitors from sitting down (and remain standing yourself)
- To bring conversations to an end in a polite but firm manner ('Sorry, I'll have to cut this short now')

If you allow yourself to become distracted from important tasks, try:

- Planning your day carefully in advance (including the breaks), so that you know exactly what you should be doing
- Rewarding yourself with a break if you can work for a certain amount of time without becoming distracted
- Organising your environment in a way that will minimise distractions
- Arranging to meet friends and colleagues for coffee or lunch if you enjoy socialising

Time-management tips

People who have learned to manage their time better say that they have made astonishing improvements by using just one or two simple techniques. Here are some steps other people have taken to overcome their problems.

- *Set aside some uninterrupted thinking and planning time each day*: use this to review your progress towards your goals and write 'to do' lists that include some of the tasks that will get you closer to your goals. This will help to make sure you spend at least part of each day working on your personal priorities.
- *Keep a clear desk*: people who are bogged down in a clutter of paperwork are not able to think clearly and many aspects of their lives suffer as a result. For a start, you will waste a lot of time and energy searching for things you have lost on a desk piled high with papers and other objects. Taking a ruthless attitude to all those papers – filing them, putting them away or throwing them in the bin – will create a calm, clear space in your mind.
- *Make better use of down time*: like sitting in a traffic jam, for example. Can you use this time to listen to an inspiring tape? Can you catch up with a backlog of routine paperwork while you are waiting for a doctor's appointment?

- *Saying no*: there are few more powerful time-management tools than being able to say 'no'. It is a difficult thing to do, partly because we want to be polite and partly because we do not want to miss out on something. Try to say 'no' in future, with a helpful suggestion and a reason. 'Sorry I can't do that for you now because I'm finishing this report for tomorrow's meeting. I could try and make time tomorrow if it's urgent.'
- *Chunking down and chunking up*: if you have a big project to tackle, break it down into small tasks. When you have lots of small tasks, practise 'chunking up'. For example you can reduce interruptions to your work flow by pulling all your outgoing phone calls together and dealing with them in a single batch.
- *Trapped in the web*: put together an internet strategy to minimise the amount of time you spend searching for

information on the web. Have a single clear objective and do not allow yourself to be distracted.

Summary

Time is a valuable resource. Your attitude towards it and the way you use it can mean the difference between tapping into your own talents or settling for a life which is shrouded in frustration. To take control of your life you have to reassess your priorities and stop blaming other people or outside circumstances for your difficulties. To make changes, step off the treadmill and begin right now – however difficult this might seem at first.

Market yourself

To achieve your goals, you will have to persuade others to buy what you have to offer – your skills, your services or your products. Completing an application form or creating a CV is no longer enough. To be sure of success it is vital to start thinking of yourself as a product or business to be marketed.

Marketing involves positioning yourself correctly – finding out who your customers are and what skills they require. It also involves making sure that your 'package' (mix of skills, experience and personal qualities) is exactly what employers want. And finally it means advertising and presenting yourself correctly.

Why marketing?

To develop an interesting and rewarding career it is not enough to wait to see what is on offer. This leaves a lot to chance and puts too many cards in the hands of the employer. To land the opportunity of a lifetime (rather than just settling for a job) it is more valuable to approach the task of selling your time and skills to a prospective employer as a marketing exercise.

The classic definition tells us that marketing involves offering the right product to the right customer at the right time in the right place and at the right price. You also have to promote the product in the right way! The idea is that you try to perceive what you have to offer (in this case you are the 'product') from the viewpoint of customers (in this case your employer or prospective employers), so that what you are giving them is what they actually require. If you can do this you will 'satisfy' their needs, and the product will sell like hot cakes.

The rest of this chapter outlines the process that we suggest you follow to market yourself effectively:

- Identify your customers
- Define what your customers want
- Analyse what you have to offer
- Establish an action plan for giving customers what they want
- Promote yourself to employers

None of this is quick and it is certainly not easy, but even carrying out some of these steps will have an enormous impact on the quality of your job applications and the way they are received.

Who are your customers?

All the work you did on Monday will help you to identify your customers – the organisations you would most like to work for.

The next step is to get to know your customers better. This can be a very time-consuming process, but it does not have to be done quickly. Knowing even a small amount about your customers will pay dividends in the end.

Collecting information about the organisations which interest you will enable you to draw up a profile of their characteristics. You will then be able to make sure that your applications are geared towards meeting their needs. At the same time you will find out exactly what you would be letting yourself in for if you accepted a job with one of those companies.

The key characteristics you need to investigate include:

- Type of industry or sector
- Business aims
- Number of employees
- Location
- How the business is structured
- Main activities and outputs
- Annual profit
- Values
- Problems and opportunities

Most of this information is easy to find on the web and in local business directories, but it is important not to accept at face value what a company says about its activities and achievements. To get a more rounded picture you will need to become an avid reader of the business sections of the local and national newspapers. And you must keep an eye on the business and management journals. Find out what the analysts are saying about the companies you want to target. Are there any big changes on the horizon? How does their performance compare with that of their competitors? How does the company treat its customers and its suppliers? And what do current and past employees of the company have to say?

This research is worthwhile because it will provide valuable clues on how to present your applications to the companies you most want to join. This information will enable you to communicate that:

- You appreciate the pressures on the organisation
- You can contribute to its future success

In addition, knowledge about the company will enable you to ask great questions if you get invited for an interview. You will look informed and inquiring and you will be in control of the conversation for a while. This will help you to make a fully-informed decision if one company makes you a job offer.

What do employers want?

Few organisations can succeed without a skilled and committed workforce. This is why many organisations will go to enormous lengths during recruitment to ensure that they select people with the knowledge, expertise and attitudes to perform their jobs to the required standard.

In the main, employers are looking for candidates who:

- Have appropriate job skills
- Are enthusiastic and willing to help
- Inspire confidence
- Can communicate effectively
- Can work with others
- Can organise themselves to achieve their objectives

If you can develop and demonstrate these skills and behaviours, you will secure your place at the top of any recruiter's selection list.

Job skills
Job skills are the specific professional and technical skills and knowledge required for a particular job. These skills vary widely, from basic word-processing skills or van driving to

knowledge of the law or carrying out surgery. People have to develop their job skills to different levels depending on the type or grade of job that they are doing.

Confidence
Confidence is a vital ingredient of a successful career. If you are confident you will inspire confidence in others and you will be able to fight your corner when it comes to getting what you want. Everything that you do and say will give the impression that you have (or lack) confidence.

Effective communication
The ability to communicate well is a vital element of success in any job. Communication is about understanding other people and enabling them to understand us. It is a two-way process and it is as much about listening and reading as it is about talking and writing.

Working with others
It does not matter if your colleagues are in the same room or scattered all over the world – you still need to be able to build positive working relationships with them. The quality of your working relationships directly affects your commitment and your ability to achieve the task in hand.

Organising yourself
To add value to any business organisation you have to be prepared to take personal responsibility for achieving your objectives. You must be able to identify your personal priorities, organise yourself and manage your time effectively.

Once you have established what prospective employers are looking for, it is time to determine what you have already so that you can work out how to fill the gaps.

Where are you now?

Managers often start their marketing research with the
SWOT (Strengths, Weaknesses, Opportunities, Threats)
technique. This helps them to clarify what they have already,
and which changes they need to make in order to satisfy
customer needs.

An individual SWOT analysis gives you a basic
understanding of the current situation and helps you to
identify what you may need to do to maximise your chances
of success. It is usually set out within the four sections of a
window, the positive points being written on the left side and
the negative ones on the right.

Strengths	Weaknesses
What have I achieved?	Are there any skills gaps?
What do I do well?	Which personal qualities do I lack?
What do I enjoy doing?	
What job skills do I have?	What do my boss, colleagues, customers complain about?
What personal qualities do I have?	
	Do I lack work experience in any area?
What resources and contacts do I have?	
	Am I able to organise myself to achieve goals?
Do I have a good track record at work?	
	What do I not enjoy doing?
Are there people who will provide me with references?	What resources and contacts do I lack?

In which situations am I most confident?	In which situations am I least confident?
Opportunities	**Threats**
Which national or local trends or changes may open up new opportunities for me?	Which trends or changes may reduce demand for my services?
Which employers need people with my skills and qualities?	What might employers be looking for that I have not got?
What are employers looking for that I might be able to supply?	With whom might I be competing in the job market?
Does new technology offer any new opportunities?	Do I always present myself in the best possible way?
How can I use what I know about effective presentation to promote myself?	

A SWOT is best done as a synthesis of other activities, so do not lose the information you collected earlier in the week. For example, you identified your contacts on Sunday, your achievements, interests, skills and personal qualities on Monday and your goals and support network on Thursday. If you have these things, note them on the left- hand side of the table, if you lack them make a note on the right.

If you do the SWOT over a period of time, the framework will generate a great deal of useful information and it may still produce some surprises. The factors you have identified determine your position in the job market. It does not matter whether the picture is positive or negative. The point is that your position can always be improved by reinforcing or strengthening the positive aspects and rectifying the negative ones.

Action planning

Your action plan should identify some objectives which:

- Build on the strengths you have identified
- Turn your weaknesses into strengths
- Make the most of opportunities
- Plan a way around the threats

If you cannot neutralise the weaknesses and threats so they do not cause too much of a problem, the only option is to live with them in the most positive way possible.

Make use of all the help and encouragement you can. Look back at your support networks to identify who can help you achieve your goal.

Some people may be helpful because they will encourage you and believe in you, others because you can share your feelings with them, others because they have specific skills, knowledge or expertise to offer.

Promoting yourself

Promoting yourself to the target companies should be an important ingredient of your action plan. You can promote yourself in a number of ways:

- Cold calling
- Creating a brilliant CV
- Writing an effective covering letter
- Projecting the right image

Cold calling
Cold calling can be an effective way of landing your dream job, but even the most confident applicants find this task extremely daunting. Contacting an employer direct rather than waiting for a job to be advertised can be time-consuming, frustrating, demoralising and downright depressing. So why do it? The answer is that, although there are plenty of places to look for vacancies (classified ads, agencies, employment centres, the internet), it can be quite

hard to get the job you want. Competition seems to increase all the time.

Start by making a list of the companies you would like to work for, then simply phone them and tell them what you can offer. Of course, it is good to do this if you have just heard on the grapevine that a particular company is short-staffed or that they need the kinds of skills and expertise that you could provide. Find out about job opportunities by keeping in regular contact with the people in your network. These days you do not have to spend hours calling each of your contacts in turn – sending messages via e-mail is much faster.

There are several things you can do to ensure that you make the very best use of any time you spend cold calling:

- Prepare your 'pitch' well. Be aware that you will only have a few minutes – maybe only a few seconds – to make an impact
- Be ready to sell yourself to whoever happens to answer the call – this could be anyone from the managing director to a departmental manager or a PA. Change your style of delivery accordingly
- Begin by saying who you are and why you are phoning. Then say what kind of job you are looking for, and why you think you would be a good candidate
- Smile when you speak
- Do not allow rejection to erode your self confidence

Your aim should be to send in a copy of your CV and ultimately to arrange a meeting where you will have the opportunity to present your skills and qualities in person.

Cold calling is not for the shrinking violet but it can be effective if you are not in a hurry to find your ideal job. Always ask for suggestions for further contacts – that way each call that you make could lead to more possibilities, any one of which could be the opening you are looking for.

Your brilliant CV

Your CV is your marketing leaflet and its purpose is to show that you are right for the job. It is vital to be able to demonstrate that you understand exactly what the employer is looking for and how you match the criteria they have set. Always think about what you are writing from the point of view of the reader. Do not be tempted to describe all of your skills and qualities in great detail in the CV, only include the most relevant information.

To create a brilliant CV:

- *Keep it short*: the rule of thumb is that your CV should never be longer than two sides of A4. You are not trying to describe your entire life history in minute detail. The aim is to show the employer that you have what they are looking for and to leave them wanting to ask you more.
- *Stand out from the crowd*: it is important to show that you are interesting and different enough to be worth interviewing. You can achieve this by developing your own style, applying colour in a subtle, elegant way and paying attention to fonts, headings and layout.
- *Choose the right format*: create a 'chronological' CV (starting with the most recent jobs and working backwards) if you want to emphasise the way that your career has developed

logically and progressively over a number of years. Create a 'functional' CV if you want to present the transferable skills that you have picked up in different roles – including work, home and leisure pursuits. Use the functional approach if you have had any career breaks or if you want to make a career change.

- *Select the right words*: it is important to work hard at presenting information in a positive, direct and personal way. Get straight to the point and do not be afraid of writing 'I' statements which bring home what your skills are and what you are capable of doing. Always choose strong, active phrases like ' I achieved', ' I created' and 'I organised'.
- *Include brief details*: write brief paragraphs on personal details, education (names of schools and colleges, dates attended and qualifications gained), training courses (and certificates gained), employment (job roles, names of employers, start and finish dates, main duties, achievements and skills), interests and references (names, job roles and contact details).
- *Do not include things like*: your age, marital status, children, weight, place of birth, state of health and national insurance number. You do not need to include GCSE grades if you went on to do A levels or a degree. Do not mention any exams you failed.
- *Make sure it looks professional*: use clear bold headings, arrange the text in neat blocks, leave wide margins and plenty of white space. Keep it simple – use bullet points to separate your ideas clearly. Avoid using lots of different fonts, italics or underlining.

Covering letter

Normally CVs sent by post should have a covering letter attached. Ignore them at your peril because they are a vitally important part of any job application. They give you a single chance to make your pitch – to capture recruiters' attention and interest so that they will turn over the page to look at your CV. If you get it right, the next step could be an interview. But if you get it wrong, your carefully crafted application could find itself very quickly on the reject pile.

Here are some key points of presentation that you need to be aware of:

- Use good quality A4 unlined white or cream paper – never be tempted to write your covering letter on your kid sister's Day-Glo orange stationery
- A word-processed letter is best because it looks business-like and you can fit more information on a page. If a handwritten letter is requested, make sure it is neat and legible
- Pay particular attention to the layout of the letter – good wide margins, addresses at the top, two or three neat paragraphs, not too much blank space at the bottom – will make your letter visually attractive so that recruiters will want to read it

Finding a personal contact in the organisation is crucial to your chance of success. If you do not know the name of the person who has advertised the vacancy, call the company and find out. Always observe the conventions: start the letter with *Dear Ms/Mr xx* and finish with *Yours sincerely*, before signing your name.

Your covering letter should be very brief, never any longer than two or three paragraphs on one side of A4. All your details should be in the CV itself – it is pointless to repeat everything in the covering letter.

Structure your letter into two or three short paragraphs which state clearly which job you are applying for, where you saw it advertised, why you are a suitable person for the job and why you want to join the organisation. Briefly summarise your main selling points.

Finally, get someone else to proofread your CV and covering letter for errors and tone before posting it, because they might notice something you have missed. Job applicants are often rejected because they have made spelling or grammatical mistakes.

Managing your impression
It is with good reason that a lot has been said and written about impression management in the past few years. Remember that your task is to convince employers that you have the job skills, the enthusiasm, the confidence and so on to help the organisation achieve its objectives. Everything that you do and say must contribute towards creating that impression. You really cannot leave it to chance because if you are not fully aware of the effect you might have on an employer you may create the wrong impression.

When you go for an interview, you cannot change your experience and your qualifications but you can control the impact that you make on the panel. Experts say that the decision to select or reject is usually taken within the first 30 seconds. This means that you may never get the chance to put right the consequences of a bad start. By consciously planning how you appear to others, you can alter the way that they respond to you and you may be able to influence their selection decisions.

Think about the messages you send to recruitment interviewers. Do you stand up straight, make eye contact and smile? If so, they will see you as confident and dynamic. However, if you look at the floor and fidget, you will be seen as indecisive and insecure.

Your clothes are a vital ingredient of your overall image so think carefully about what they say about you. The key word here is appropriateness – are they the right clothes for this company, for this job, for the interview and for you? Do they represent the right mix of creativity and formality? It is not just the style of clothes that is important, your choice and mix of colours also sends powerful messages.

Remember, how you are perceived is up to you. Ask a friend what impression you make with your clothes, general appearance and body language and then work to alter those outward signals. You will be surprised at how much you can say about yourself without saying a single word!

Summary

This final section has sought to encourage you to take a new perspective on all of the positive qualities that you have to offer. It has drawn together many of the threads that we have covered this week, and shows how you can use what you know about yourself and about the job market to present and promote yourself appropriately to suitable employers.

And finally . . .

Remember that a career for life no longer exists, and that employers can no longer promise anyone continuous employment – even to those who perform well. Taking personal responsibility for your own future helps you to develop the work habits you need for job success, while at the same time preparing your mind for self-employment.

What you have to do is trust in the future and have confidence in your ability to survive and prosper – no matter what fate has in store.